CHANGING
DOMESTIC
PRIORITIES

John L. Palmer and Isabel V. Sawhill, Series Editors

# WAGE INFLATION

## PROSPECTS FOR DECELERATION

Wayne Vroman

# WAGE
# INFLATION

# THE CHANGING DOMESTIC PRIORITIES SERIES

Listed below are the titles published to date in the Changing Domestic Priorities Series

# WAGE
# INFLATION

## PROSPECTS
## FOR
## DECELERATION

*Wayne Vroman*

The Changing Domestic Priorities Series
John L. Palmer and Isabel V. Sawhill, Editors

THE URBAN INSTITUTE PRESS · WASHINGTON, D.C.

THE URBAN INSTITUTE is a nonprofit policy research and educational organization established in Washington, D.C. in 1968. Its staff investigates the social and economic problems confronting the nation and government policies and programs designed to alleviate such problems. The Institute disseminates significant findings of its research through the publications program of its Press. The Institute has two goals for work in each of its research areas: to help shape thinking about societal problems and efforts to solve them, and to improve government decisions and performance by providing better information and analytic tools.

Through work that ranges from broad conceptual studies to administrative and technical assistance, Institute researchers contribute to the stock of knowledge available to public officials and to private individuals and groups concerned with formulating and implementing more efficient and effective government policy.

Conclusions or opinions expressed in Institute publications are those of the authors and do not necessarily reflect the views of other staff members, officers or trustees of the Institute, or of any organizations which provide financial support to the Institute.

# CONTENTS

## TABLES

## FIGURE

# FOREWORD

This report is part of the "Changing Domestic Priorities" project of The Urban Institute. This project is examining the shifts that are occurring in the nation's economic and social policies under the Reagan administration and analyzing the effect of these changes on people, places, and institutions.

A central priority for the country and the administration has been to bring inflation under control. Any long-lasting improvement on this front requires a slowdown in wage growth. This paper documents the extent to which this slowdown has occurred, where it has occurred, and the reasons for its occurrence.

Comparing the most recent period since the 1981-1982 recession began to the record for the previous two years, Vroman notes that deceleration in money wage growth has been about three percentage points.

Some observers believe that this much progress is unusual and cite one of two factors as being responsible: (1) fundamental changes in collective bargaining practices because of more aggressive management behavior, growth in nonunion employment, and import competition or (2) replacement of stop-go monetary policies with a more consistent and credible commitment to slower monetary growth. Other experts argue that the higher level of unemployment and lagged effects of an earlier decline in overall inflation connected with oil and food prices fully explain the reduction in wage inflation.

Using a variety of evidence, Vroman tested these different hypotheses and found the following. First, although wage increases negotiated in recent major collective bargaining agreements have slowed dramatically, they are still increasing at about the same pace as wages in the nonunion sector. Furthermore, although conces-

ix

sions and some breakdown of industrywide bargaining have occurred, two important features of union wage setting, multiyear
contracts and escalator clauses, emerged with only minor changes
in 1982 contract negotiations. Thus, the potential for large future
union wage increases still exists. Second, the recent slowdown in
economywide compensation increases has not been much greater
than one would expect based on the higher unemployment and reduced price inflation that have prevailed in recent quarters. The
recent deceleration, however, has been a little larger than expected,
suggesting that a more credible monetary policy or a new collective
bargaining environment may also be contributing in a minor way
to the slowdown.


John L. Palmer
Isabel V. Sawhill
General Editors
Changing Domestic Priorities Series

# ABOUT THE AUTHOR

WAYNE VROMAN is a senior research associate and member of the Human Resources Policy Center at The Urban Institute. He is the author of several papers on wage inflation and unemployment. His work on wage inflation has included evaluations of incomes policies and studies of union wage dynamics.

CHAPTER 1

# INTRODUCTION

Poor macroeconomic performance by the U.S. economy during the decade of the 1970s was manifested in many different ways. Compared to the previous decade, real output grew more slowly, average inflation rates and unemployment were both much higher, and the rate of labor productivity growth slowed noticeably. The central policy question that emerged was how to achieve full resource utilization at a low (or zero) rate of inflation. During the last three years of the 1960s and 1970s average inflation rates were 4.2 percent and 8.5 percent respectively, while unemployment rates averaged 3.6 percent and 6.3 percent.[1]

Exogenous increases in the prices of petroleum products, other raw materials, and agricultural products made important contributions to the economy's poor inflationary performance. It was also clear, however, that after these price shocks occurred inflation rates remained at high levels even in the face of sizeable declines in overall resource utilization. Terms such as stagflation, inflationary momentum, wage stickiness, and wage norms were coined to describe the inflationary phenomena of the 1970s. New theories emerged that stressed the importance of inflationary expectations in explaining the persistence of inflation in the face of restrictive macro policies. As the newer theories gained adherents, disputes about the proper way to formulate and conduct macro policy became more heated. Increased emphasis was placed on the importance of monetary policy

[The author of this paper is grateful to Larry Slifman and Robert Solow for helpful comments on an earlier draft. Funding for this study was provided by a consortium of foundations and corporations, principally The Ford Foundation and the John D. and Catherine T. MacArthur Foundation.]

1

as skepticism about fiscal policy's ability to control inflation became widespread.

Prices in the economy's industrial sector are strongly influenced by costs. Since labor costs account for more than two-thirds of total costs, they are of particular importance if macro policy is to successfully slow the pace of inflation. During the 1970s, unit labor cost increases were unusually high because wages (and other components of labor compensation) increased more rapidly and because the rate of labor productivity growth decreased. Of these two factors, accelerated growth in hourly compensation was quantitatively more significant. Annual gains in hourly compensation averaged 6.5 percent and 8.6 percent in 1967-1969 and 1977-1979 respectively (an increase of 2.1 percent), while the corresponding average annual productivity gains were 1.6 percent and .4 percent respectively (a decrease of 1.2 percent).

This paper focuses on recent inflationary experiences as manifested in the behavior of money wage changes. Its purpose is threefold: (1) to describe overall wage trends since 1970; (2) to examine and interpret quarterly wage changes since January 1979; and (3) to assess the likely course of wage inflation through the end of 1983. The paper is intended to be a nontechnical summary of both recent developments and the likely near-term prospects for aggregate wage inflation.

CHAPTER 2

# STAGFLATION OF THE 1970s

The traditional way of reducing inflation is to depress the overall rate of resource utilization. In the labor market, Phillips curves
estimated from historical data have provided policy makers with
estimates of the trade-off between the rate of change of money wages
and the unemployment rate. Since 1969, unfortunately, increases
in unemployment have not yielded much in terms of reduced wage
inflation.

Figure 1 is a graphic illustration of the "shifting Phillips curve,"
which has received so much attention during the 1970s. The figure
is a scatter diagram showing annual rates of wage inflation and
unemployment rates for the years 1953 to 1981. During this twenty-
nine year interval, there were six major downturns in economic
activity.[1] The solid lines in the figure show the time paths of annual
wage inflation and unemployment during each of these downturns.

In the first three recessionary episodes (1953-1954, 1957-1958,
and 1960-1961) the rate of wage change decelerated in the face of
higher unemployment. A wage inflation-unemployment trade-off is
apparent during these periods. Although wage inflation decelerated
only modestly in 1960-1961 (from 3.3 to 2.8 percent), there was also
a much smaller increase in unemployment than in the two previous
recessions.

Two aspects of later recessions contrast with the earlier downturns. (1) Increasingly higher levels of both unemployment and wage
inflation are observed for the initial years of these periods. Inflation
and unemployment were both higher in 1973 than in 1969, and both
were again higher in 1979 than in 1973. The data configurations
provide empirical support for assertions about outward shifts of the

3

FIGURE 1

UNEMPLOYMENT AND MONEY WAGE CHANGES, 1953 TO 1981

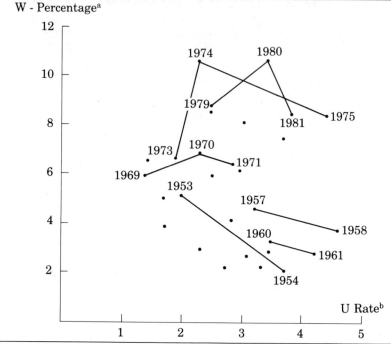

SOURCE:   All data published by the U.S. Department of Labor, Bureau of Labor Statistics.

   a.  W - Annual percentage increases in a fixed weight index of straight time hourly earnings in manufacturing. Increases measured from December to December.
   b.  U Rate - Unemployment rate for white men aged 35–54, annual average.

Phillips curve during the 1970s. (2) Most startling is the positive association between unemployment changes and changes in wage inflation in the first year of higher unemployment. Higher unemployment was associated with higher, not lower, wage inflation during 1970, 1974, and 1980. In each of these years, especially 1974 and 1980, the economy was experiencing substantial price inflation. Catch-up responses of wages to higher price inflation were undoubtedly contributing to increased wage inflation in these years.[2] In the second year of higher unemployment (1971, 1975, and 1981) wage inflation did decelerate, but it still equaled or exceeded the inflation rate of the prerecession year. Thus, for each of the three periods, restrictive macro policy was able to reduce overall resource utilization and increase unemployment, but this did not yield anything in terms of a measurably reduced (peak to trough) rate of money wage inflation. The episodes depicted in figure 1 are a dramatic representation of the economy's recent stagflationary behavior.

# CHAPTER 3

# ANNUAL MONEY WAGE CHANGES, 1965 TO 1981

Figure 1 illustrated that money wages have behaved perversely in each of the last three recessions. To provide more detailed documentation on wage developments during this unusual period of recent economic history, table 1 displays selected annual wage inflation series for the years 1965 to 1981.[1] All series in the table show that money wages were rising much more rapidly in 1979-1981 than in the years before 1970. Wage increases clearly accelerated between 1965 and 1969. The two years of highest wage inflation were 1974 and 1980. It is also obvious that union wage increases (columns (5) and (10)) decelerated rapidly during 1972 when Phase II of the Nixon administration's wage-price controls was in effect. Rapid union wage gains in 1974 coincide with the ending of controls. Finally, note that wage inflation during 1981 was somewhat lower than during 1980.

The data in table 1 have been arranged to address the following questions: (1) Have union wage increases been unusually rapid in recent years? (2) Have union wage increases contributed to the unusual behavior of overall wage changes in recent recessionary periods? Table 1 indicates that both questions should be answered affirmatively, with some qualifications.[2] Union settlements played an active role as a source of inflationary impulses during the 1970-1971 recession. In 1974-1975 and 1980-1981 high union wage increases were also observed in a recessionary environment, but much of the increase was an automatic response because of cost-of-living escalator clauses that perpetuated earlier price increases. During these two periods union wages certainly increased but more in response to price inflation rather than as an initiating cause of price inflation.

TABLE 1

SELECTED MEASURES OF ANNUAL PERCENTAGE WAGE CHANGES, 1965 TO 1981

| Year | Hourly Earnings Index, Private Nonfarm[a] | | | Scheduled Wage Adjustments, Manufacturing[b] | | | Employment Cost Index (Wages and Salaries) Private Nonfarm[c] | | | Major Agreements, Effective Wage Adjustments, Private Nonfarm[d] |
|---|---|---|---|---|---|---|---|---|---|---|
| | All Industries (1) | High Unionization Industries (2) | Low Unionization Industries (3) | All Workers (4) | Union Workers (5) | Nonunion Workers (6) | All Workers (7) | Union Workers (8) | Nonunion Workers (9) | (10) |
| 1965 | 3.5 | 3.4 | 3.4 | 3.0 | 2.9 | 3.2 | — | — | — | — |
| 1966 | 4.9 | 4.1 | 6.1 | 3.3 | 3.2 | 3.9 | — | — | — | — |
| 1967 | 5.3 | 5.0 | 5.7 | 4.0 | 4.0 | 4.6 | — | — | — | — |
| 1968 | 6.8 | 6.7 | 6.9 | 5.0 | 5.0 | 5.0 | — | — | — | 6.0 |
| 1969 | 6.6 | 6.6 | 6.5 | 5.1 | 5.3 | 4.6 | — | — | — | 6.5 |
| 1970 | 6.8 | 6.9 | 6.6 | 6.0 | 6.4 | 4.7 | — | — | — | 8.8 |
| 1971 | 7.1 | 7.6 | 6.6 | 6.4 | 7.1 | 4.0 | — | — | — | 9.2 |
| 1972 | 6.4 | 6.7 | 5.9 | 5.1 | 5.4 | 4.4 | — | — | — | 6.6 |
| 1973 | 6.5 | 6.5 | 6.5 | 6.3 | 6.4 | 6.0 | — | — | — | 7.0 |
| 1974 | 9.2 | 10.0 | 8.5 | 8.4 | 8.7 | 7.7 | — | — | — | 9.4 |
| 1975 | 7.1 | 7.9 | 6.4 | 7.4 | 8.1 | 5.9 | — | — | — | 8.7 |
| 1976 | 7.4 | 7.6 | 7.3 | 7.3 | 7.8 | 6.1 | 7.2 | 8.2 | 6.8 | 8.1 |
| 1977 | 7.4 | 7.7 | 7.0 | 7.2 | 7.7 | 6.0 | 7.0 | 7.5 | 6.5 | 8.0 |
| 1978 | 8.5 | 8.4 | 8.6 | 7.6 | 8.0 | 6.8 | 7.6 | 8.0 | 7.6 | 8.2 |
| 1979 | 8.3 | 8.5 | 8.0 | — | — | — | 8.7 | 9.0 | 8.5 | 9.1 |
| 1980 | 9.3 | 9.9 | 8.8 | — | — | — | 9.0 | 10.9 | 8.1 | 9.9 |
| 1981 | 8.2 | 8.5 | 8.0 | — | — | — | 8.8 | 9.6 | 8.5 | 9.5 |

| | | | | | | | | | |
|---|---|---|---|---|---|---|---|---|---|
| 1970-1981 Average | 7.7 | 8.0 | 7.4 | 6.9e | 7.3e | 5.7e | 8.0g | 8.9g | 7.7g | 8.5 |
| 1970-1975 Average | 7.2 | 7.6 | 6.8 | 6.6 | 7.0 | 5.4 | — | — | — | 8.3 |
| 1976-1981 Average | 8.2 | 8.4 | 8.0 | 7.4f | 7.8f | 6.3f | 8.0 | 8.9 | 7.7 | 8.8 |

a. Based on the BLS index of average hourly earnings. Hourly earnings are measured net of interindustry changes in employment and net of overtime pay in manufacturing. Annual changes are based on December to December comparisons. High union industries are mining, construction, manufacturing, transportation, and public utilities (SIC codes 10-49). Low union industries are wholesale and retail trade, finance, and services (SIC codes 50-89).

b. Based on the former BLS survey of Wage Developments in Manufacturing (WDM). This survey was discontinued after 1978. Excluded from these data are unscheduled wage increases such as year end bonuses and merit pay increases. Median increases are shown for 1965-1968 while mean increases are shown for later years.

c. Based on the BLS employment cost index (ECI) of wage and salary payments. Estimated annual increases are based on comparisons of the index for the fourth quarter (December) with the fourth quarter (December) of the preceding year.

d. Effective wage changes in major collective bargaining situations; i.e., those covering 1,000 or more workers. This is the sum of wage changes negotiated in new agreements, deferred increases from prior years negotiations and cost-of-living increases.

e. Average for the nine years 1970-1978.

f. Average for the three years 1976-1978.

g. Average for the six years 1976-1981.

The bottom lines of table 1 summarize information useful for comparing union with nonunion wage increases. For all pairwise comparisons that can be made, union wage increases exceed nonunion increases,[3] and increases in highly unionized industries exceed those of low unionization industries. All wage series increased more rapidly in 1976-1981 than in the earlier 1970-1975 period. There are suggestions, however, that the differential between union and nonunion increases was larger in the earlier period.[4] Thus, the independent contribution of union settlements to overall wage inflation appears to have been more important in the first half of the 1970s than in 1976-1981. For the 1970-1981 period as a whole, union wages clearly increased more rapidly than nonunion wages.[5]

To provide more insight into union wage behavior during the three most recent recessions, table 2 displays information on wage changes in major union agreements. Major agreements are those where the bargaining unit has at least 1,000 workers. They cover about 10 million workers, or roughly half of all unionized workers in the private nonfarm economy. The very largest bargaining situations that receive so much attention from policy makers and the media are all included in these data.

Table 2 focuses both on the total size and the composition of the wage increases in the major agreements. Fixed (or noncontingent) increases are stipulated at the time of contract signing. Since most workers are covered by multiyear contracts, current settlements and deferred increases from earlier settlements are both components of the fixed increases in a given calendar year. Cost-of-living (COL or contingent) adjustments from escalator clauses are the other component of the total wage change. Between 1968 and 1981 COL coverage increased, and payments under escalator formulas became more generous. Thus, the escalator component became increasingly important in the overall compensation packages of these union workers. Since 1978, COL adjustments have accounted for about 30 percent of the total effective wage changes compared to only 5 percent in the late 1960s.

Details on average escalator adjustments appear in columns (5)-(9). Payout formulas are typically of the cents-per-point variety (e.g., 1 cent for each .3 change in the CPI), with quarterly reviews and a short payout lag.[6] During the early 1970s the average COL yield (the ratio of percentage COL increases to price increases) increased as maximum adjustments or "caps" were removed from many escalator provisions. Since 1975, yields have averaged about .60. No-

TABLE 2

COMPONENTS OF EFFECTIVE WAGE CHANGES IN MAJOR COLLECTIVE BARGAINING AGREEMENTS, 1968 TO 1981

| Year | Total (1) | Fixed Adjustments (First Year and Deferred Increases) (2) | COL Adjustments (3) | COL/Total (=(3)/(1)) (4) | Annual Inflation Rate[b] (percentage) (5) | Average COL Increase[a] (percentage) (6) | Average COL Yield (=(6)/(5)) (7) | Proportion with COL Increases[a] (8) | Effective COL Yield (=(7).(8) =(3)/(5)) (9) |
|---|---|---|---|---|---|---|---|---|---|
| 1968 | 6.0 | 5.7 | .3 | .05 | 4.7 | 1.6 | .34 | .21 | .06 |
| 1969 | 6.5 | 6.2 | .3 | .05 | 5.6 | 1.6 | .29 | .21 | .05 |
| 1970 | 8.8 | 8.2 | .6 | .07 | 5.8 | 3.7 | .64 | .17 | .10 |
| 1971 | 9.2 | 8.5 | .7 | .08 | 3.6 | 3.1 | .86 | .20 | .19 |
| 1972 | 6.6 | 5.9 | .7 | .11 | 3.4 | 2.0 | .59 | .36 | .21 |
| 1973 | 7.0 | 5.7 | 1.3 | .19 | 7.9 | 4.1 | .52 | .31 | .16 |
| 1974 | 9.4 | 7.4 | 1.9 | .20 | 12.0 | 5.8 | .48 | .33 | .16 |
| 1975 | 8.7 | 6.5 | 2.2 | .25 | 7.6 | 4.8 | .63 | .47 | .29 |
| 1976 | 8.1 | 6.4 | 1.6 | .20 | 5.3 | 3.5 | .66 | .45 | .30 |
| 1977 | 8.0 | 6.2 | 1.7 | .21 | 6.5 | 3.9 | .60 | .43 | .26 |
| 1978 | 8.2 | 5.7 | 2.4 | .29 | 8.9 | 5.0 | .56 | .48 | .27 |
| 1979 | 9.1 | 6.0 | 3.1 | .34 | 12.2 | 6.8 | .56 | .45 | .25 |
| 1980 | 9.9 | 7.1 | 2.8 | .28 | 12.6 | 7.7 | .61 | .37 | .22 |
| 1981 | 9.5 | 6.3 | 3.2 | .31 | 10.2 | 6.1 | .60 | .54 | .31 |

a. Based on BLS data that appear periodically in *Current Wage Developments*.
b. Based on twelve-month changes in the all items CPI between October and October of the previous year.

ticeable increases in the proportion who actually received COL payments occurred in 1972 (mainly among steelworkers), 1975 (among teamsters, communications workers, and coal miners) and 1981 (for reasons not obvious to the author). On average .45 of these workers have been receiving COL increases in the years since 1975. The effective yields shown in the last column combine information on both average yields and coverage to show what portion of each year's inflation was automatically fed back into the wage adjustments of workers covered by major agreements. Since 1975, effective yields have ranged from .22 to .31 and averaged .27. Thus, COL adjustments that have provided partial inflation protection assumed an important (but still a minority) role in union wage changes during the 1970s.

The configuration of major union wage changes was much different in the downturn of 1969-1971 than in the two recessions following the oil price shocks of 1973 and 1979. Effective wage changes increased from 6.5 percent in 1969 to 8.8 percent in 1970 and to 9.2 percent in 1971. Fixed wage increases accounted for most of this wage acceleration, 2.3 of the 2.7 percentage point increase between 1969 and 1971. Major union wage gains rose noticeably, exceeded current inflation rates, and occurred despite a large increase in overall unemployment. This unprecedented behavior of wages in the major agreements led policy makers to impose a ninety-day wage and price freeze in August 1971, the first phase of an incomes policy that lasted until April 1974. The large wage settlements reached in the major agreements (particularly the automobile settlement of November 1970 and the steel settlement of August 1971) were a major cause of the stagflation that the economy experienced in 1970-1971.

When price increases accelerated in 1973-1974 and again in 1978-1980, COL adjustments played a much more important role in the upward movement of wages in the major agreements. In both episodes the rates of price inflation exceeded the wage adjustments paid to these workers (compare columns (1) and (5) in 1973, 1974, 1978, 1979, and 1980), and thus their real wages fell despite larger fixed wage increases and larger COL adjustments. On average, workers in the major agreements were more effective than other (smaller union and nonunion) workers in preventing erosion of their real wages. Thus, their relative wage continued to rise despite the partial nature of the inflation protection provided by escalator arrangements and a decline in their real wages.[7]   In these episodes wages in the major agreements could be characterized as trying to keep up with the tempo of the inflationary parade whereas in 1970-1971 they acted more like a stubborn drum major leading the parade and refusing to slow down.

CHAPTER 4

# RECENT QUARTERLY WAGE TRENDS

The annual data just examined suggest there was some slow-down in wage inflation during 1981. Rates of increase in the various wage series, however, ranged from 8.0 to 9.6 percent, far above the rates required for a permanent, large scale reduction in the economy's overall inflation rate.

Since the timing of wage and price accelerations and decelerations can be pinpointed more precisely with quarterly data, table 3 displays selected quarterly wage inflation series for the period 1979I to 1982II[1] along with data on unemployment and price inflation. Unemployment rates remained on two plateaus for most of these quarters (at about 6 percent from 1979I to 1980I and at 7.4 percent from 1980II to 1981III) and then moved upward in the last three quarters to 8.4, 8.8, and 9.5 percent respectively. Real GNP reductions in 1980II and again in 1981IV-1982II coincide perfectly with the increases in the unemployment rate.

Two price inflation series are displayed in table 3 to provide insight into the importance of particular markets in recent price developments. The special index in column (3) is offered as a proxy for the underlying inflation rate, while the all items CPI in column (2) reflects underlying price movements as well as developments in three markets with extremely volatile inflation rates: energy, food, and housing. During the eight quarters of 1979 and 1980 price inflation in these three markets caused average increases in the all items CPI to exceed the special index by half, 12.9 versus 8.6 percent. Mortgage interest rates and energy prices increased especially rapidly during this period.

15

TABLE 3

QUARTERLY WAGE AND PRICE CHANGES SINCE 1979[a]

| Year | Unemployment Rate[b,d] (1) | Inflation Rate CPI[c,d] | | Hourly Earnings Index[d] | | | Employment Cost Index[d] (Wages and Salaries) | | | Major Agreements Effective Wage Adjustments[d] (10) |
|---|---|---|---|---|---|---|---|---|---|---|
| | | All Items (2) | Special Index[f] (3) | All Industries (4) | High Union Industries (5) | Low Union Industries (6) | All Workers (7) | Union Workers (8) | Non-union Workers (9) | |
| Average for the 1970s | 6.2 | 7.1 | 6.0 | 7.5 | 7.8 | 7.1 | 7.6[e] | 8.2[e] | 7.4[e] | 8.3 |
| 1979I | 5.9 | 12.8 | 6.8 | 7.2 | 5.3 | 9.4 | 8.2 | 7.3 | 8.7 | 5.7 |
| 1979II | 5.7 | 15.1 | 8.3 | 6.2 | 8.1 | 4.2 | 8.0 | 8.7 | 8.0 | 10.8 |
| 1979III | 5.8 | 13.2 | 7.2 | 12.0 | 13.1 | 10.9 | 8.9 | 9.0 | 7.8 | 13.9 |
| 1979IV | 6.0 | 12.2 | 7.7 | 7.8 | 8.2 | 6.6 | 9.7 | 10.9 | 9.6 | 6.6 |
| 1980I | 6.3 | 18.4 | 11.3 | 9.5 | 6.8 | 12.3 | 10.0 | 9.6 | 10.4 | 6.6 |
| 1980II | 7.3 | 13.7 | 8.7 | 8.3 | 10.1 | 5.6 | 8.8 | 11.3 | 7.3 | 13.9 |
| 1980III | 7.7 | 6.8 | 10.9 | 10.3 | 12.4 | 8.0 | 9.0 | 12.4 | 7.2 | 14.8 |
| 1980IV | 7.4 | 11.1 | 8.3 | 9.3 | 10.4 | 8.4 | 8.4 | 10.2 | 7.5 | 5.3 |
| 1981I | 7.4 | 10.8 | 8.3 | 10.0 | 6.9 | 13.4 | 11.4 | 6.8 | 13.7 | 7.0 |
| 1981II | 7.4 | 9.7 | 10.0 | 6.4 | 8.6 | 4.0 | 8.4 | 11.1 | 7.5 | 13.4 |
| 1981III | 7.4 | 12.3 | 11.8 | 11.6 | 12.2 | 11.0 | 8.2 | 11.2 | 6.6 | 13.9 |

TABLE 3 (continued)

QUARTERLY WAGE AND PRICE CHANGES SINCE 1979[a]

| Year | Unemployment Rate[b,d] (1) | Inflation Rate CPI[c,d] | | Hourly Earnings Index[d] | | | Employment Cost Index[d] (Wages and Salaries) | | | Major Agreements Effective Wage Adjustments[d] (10) |
|---|---|---|---|---|---|---|---|---|---|---|
| | | All Items (2) | Special Index[f] (3) | All Industries (4) | High Union Industries (5) | Low Union Industries (6) | All Workers (7) | Union Workers (8) | Non-union Workers (9) | |
| 1981IV | 8.4 | 3.2 | 7.4 | 5.1 | 6.5 | 3.7 | 7.2 | 9.3 | 6.4 | 6.1 |
| 1982I | 8.8 | 2.3 | 5.4 | 5.5 | 4.5 | 6.7 | 8.3 | 5.8 | 9.6 | 4.1 |
| 1982II | 9.5 | 11.0 | 7.6 | 6.0 | 6.7 | 5.1 | 4.6 | 6.1 | 3.5 | 8.2 |

a. All wage and price increases are measured from seasonally unadjusted data for the final months of the quarter in question. Quarterly percentage increases are measured at annual rates.

b. Unemployment rate for persons 16 and older, seasonally adjusted.

c. Consumer Price Index for all urban consumers.

d. Based on regularly published U.S. Department of Labor-BLS data.

e. Averages for the four years 1976-1979.

f. CPI less food, energy, home purchases, and finance.

The contrast between the two inflation series has been smaller during 1981 and 1982, although sharp differences are apparent for individual quarters. When food and energy prices declined in 1981IV and 1982I, the all items CPI advanced at 2 to 3 percent annual rates. Rapid inflation followed in 1982II. During these three most recent quarters the special index increased at annual rates in the 5.5-7.5 percent range. Compared to 1980I-1981III, the special index has been increasing at a slower pace in these most recent quarters.[2]

If inflation is to move downward in a sustained manner, it is necessary to reduce the rate of money wage changes. The present recession is already providing evidence of a deceleration in money wage growth. A deceleration is apparent in all three wage series displayed in table 3. Quarterly data from the hourly earnings index give definite evidence of a slowdown, with percentage increases in the all industry series averaging 5.5 percent during 1981IV-1982II compared to an average of 9.3 percent in the seven preceding quarters. The slowdown is present in both the high union and the low union industries. Since the table 3 data are not seasonally adjusted, comparisons should be with corresponding quarters in earlier years. For the all industry index, percentage wage increases averaged 8.5 in 1979IV-1980II and 8.6 in 1980IV-1981II compared to 5.5 in 1981IV-1982II. Thus, a sizeable slowdown of roughly three percentage points is observed for the three most recent quarters.

Columns (5) and (6) show clearly that union and nonunion wage increases follow distinct seasonal patterns. Nonunion wage increases are concentrated in the first quarter of each year, while union increases are higher in the later quarters and particularly in the third quarter. For the fourteen calendar quarters covered by the table, wage increases in the less unionized industries exceed increases for the highly unionized industries in each of the four first quarters but then are consistently lower in each of the ten other quarters. Consequently, the small acceleration of wage gains in the less unionized industries observed in 1982I reflects a seasonal pattern and is entirely consistent with an overall slowdown in nonunion wage increases.[3]

Data from the employment cost index (ECI) also point to a recent slowdown in money wage inflation. Columns (7), (8), and (9) of table 3 show that wage changes for all workers, union workers, and non-union workers were lower in 1981IV-1982II than the average for the seven preceding quarters. For the three groups the average extent of wage deceleration in the last three quarters relative to the preceding seven was 2.5, 3.3, and 2.1 percent respectively. When the last three quarters are compared to 1979IV-1980II and 1980IV-1981II, the magnitude of the deceleration is just less than 3 percentage points for all three groups.[4]

Union wages determined by the major collective bargaining agreements also have decelerated noticeably in recent quarters. Column (10) shows that effective wage changes follow highly seasonal patterns with second and third quarter increases being much larger than first and fourth quarter increases. Wage changes during the first two quarters of 1982 were 2.9 and 5.2 percentage points below the increases of the corresponding 1981 quarters.[5]

To summarize, money wages definitely increased more slowly during 1981IV-1982II than in preceding quarters. The size of the wage deceleration has been about 3 percentage points in the hourly earnings index, a little less than 3 percentage points in the employment cost index and more than 3 percentage points in wages determined by major collective bargaining agreements.

Wage inflation patterns during the downturns of 1980II and 1981IV-1982II present sharp contrasts. In both instances real GNP fell by about 2.5 percent.[6] Also, in both cases the unemployment rate rose substantially, by 1.4 percentage points between 1980I and 1980III and by 2.1 percentage points between 1981III and 1982II. During the 1980 downturn there was no strong evidence of a (simultaneous or lagged) slowdown in the growth of money wages. The various money wage series shown in table 3 were increasing almost as rapidly in 1980III-IV as they had been in 1979III-IV even though unemployment was about 1.5 percentage points higher.

When unemployment increased in 1981IV-1982II, there was an instantaneous and sizeable deceleration in money wage growth. At this writing the slowdown in money wage growth for these three quarters appears to be about 3 percentage points. The wages determined by major collective bargaining agreements may be exhibiting a substantially larger deceleration. Better estimates of the exact size of the wage deceleration can be made when data for 1982III and 1982IV become available.

Alternative explanations can be suggested for the contrasting behavior of wage inflation in the two downturns. One follows directly from the modified Phillips curve literature where wage inflation moves inversely with the unemployment rate but positively with the rate of price inflation.[7] Note in table 3 that the average rate of price inflation (as measured by the all items CPI) decelerated sharply starting in 1981IV whereas in 1980 it continued to advance at nearly a double digit rate into the third and fourth quarters of the year. The current and lagged effects of price inflation on wage growth would have worked against the effects of higher unemployment in 1980 whereas in 1981-1982 they would have reenforced the effects of increased unemployment. Thus, in the most recent quarters higher unemployment is clearly associated with a deceleration of money wage gains. The next chapter discusses more fully alternative explanations for the recent wage deceleration.

CHAPTER 5

# INTERPRETATIONS OF RECENT WAGE TRENDS

A slowdown in the rate of money wage inflation has occurred in all the wage series displayed in table 3. The deceleration was noticeable in 1981IV and a larger slowdown is apparent in the first half of 1982. At least three explanations can be offered for the recent deceleration of money wage increases. Respectively these can be characterized as (1) the modified Phillips curve explanation, (2) the change-in-wage-bargaining explanation, and (3) the credible policy of monetary restraint explanation.[1]

## Three Explanations for the Recent Wage Deceleration

The mainline wage inflation literature and the large scale econometric models both employ a modified Phillips curve to explain money wage dynamics. Unemployment (or some other index of excess labor demand) and the (expected or lagged) inflation rate are the main explanatory variables, but the effects of other factors such as profits, personal tax rates, the minimum wage, and incomes policies have also been analyzed. Empirical estimates of modified Phillips curves proliferated in the 1970s. The general finding was (1) the impact of unemployment on wage change decreased, (2) the impact of past inflation increased, and (3) past inflation had a lagged effect on wages for a longer time period in comparison to equations fitted to earlier data, that is, data through the late 1960s. In short the equations evolved so that money wage changes became less sensitive to unemployment and more responsive to inflation. In re-

cent quarters both variables have changed in ways that would cause
modified Phillips curve equations to predict a lower rate of money
wage inflation. The accuracy of these predictions will be explored
later under "Wage Equation Forecasts for 1981 and 1982."

Some labor economists have recently argued that collective bargaining in the early 1980s is in an important transition period. After
thirty years of comparative stability in the structure of collective
bargaining, changes are taking place that, among other things, will
result in much lower union wage settlements now and in the foreseeable future. The combined effects of more aggressive management bargaining behavior, growth in nonunion employment, and
import competition will sharply limit the ability of union negotiators
to obtain large multiyear wage packages. If true, this would mark
a major change from the 1970s when settlements in major situations
consistently exceeded nonunion wage increases (see table 1). Early
contract renegotiations, wage and work rule concessions, and a
breakdown of strict pattern bargaining within several industries
are all cited as evidence in support of this argument.

The thesis that collective bargaining is undergoing major changes
is controversial.[2] Some view recent developments as a combination
of recession-induced responses and idiosyncratic patterns in a few
major industries. Under this latter interpretation large multiyear
wage settlements will return once the economy rebounds and be a
source of inflationary problems in future years. To prevent a recur-
rence of rapid wage inflation from this sector of the labor market,
new forms of union wage determination may be required, that is,
gain sharing, shorter contract durations, and reduced wage payments under escalator clauses.

Full confirmation or rejection of the change-in-wage-bargaining
hypothesis must await a return to full employment and associated
data on settlements reached at that time. When the 1982 wage
outcomes in the largest collective bargaining situations are examined, it is clear they are much smaller than outcomes from the
preceding bargaining round. Less clear are the reasons for this and
the size of the effect on aggregate wage changes. Details of these
settlements will be discussed under "Recent Union Contract Settlements."

The Reagan administration is placing heavy reliance on monetary restraint to retard the rates of wage and price inflation. The
administration and the Fed believe that restraint on the growth of
money and credit will exert continued downward pressure on the

inflation rate. It is further believed by some Reagan administration economists and by a substantial number of so-called monetarist economists that consistent control of monetary growth will produce better inflationary performance than a monetary policy that also incorporates interest rate considerations. Consistent and slow monetary growth, it is argued, will reduce inflationary expectations and will achieve reductions in actual inflation more effectively than a so-called stop-go monetary policy that tries to counteract the ups and downs in real economic activity and inflation.[3]

The Fed has had money growth targets for several years. In October 1979 new operating procedures for the conduct of monetary policy were instituted. These were intended to achieve greater short-term control over money and credit growth through control of non-borrowed reserves. Although short-run monetary growth has remained difficult to control, the Fed has been largely successful in achieving its monetary growth targets in 1981 and 1982.[4]

During the recent period of monetary restraint the expected rate of price inflation as measured in two separate surveys (the Livingston index and Michigan's Survey of Consumer Finances) has been reduced. Expected annual inflation rates in the CPI declined from 10.3 to 5.7 percent between December 1980 and June 1982 (Livingston data) and from 7.7 to 4.7 percent between 1981I and 1982II (Michigan data).[5]

Other factors besides slow growth in monetary aggregates have contributed to the recent slowdown in inflationary expectations. Econometric analyses of measured inflationary expectations, for example, the Livingston or the Michigan series, point to the importance of recent actual price changes as determinants of expected price changes.[6] Actual price changes themselves respond not only to lagged price changes and to monetary growth but also to supply shocks in agriculture and energy as well as the overall level of resource utilization. The studies of inflationary expectations consistently show that lagged growth in the money stock affects expectations even after controlling for the effects of actual inflation and other factors.[7] Since there have been only a few years of experience under the Fed policy of targeted monetary growth, it is still too early to determine whether or not this policy is having even stronger effects on price expectations than the previous policy. One possible manifestation of stronger effects in the labor market would be a lower rate of money wage inflation for each observed rate of actual price inflation, that is, overpredictions of actual wage inflation.

## Recent Union Contract Settlements

The change-in-wage-bargaining hypothesis can be explored by noting the 1982 settlements reached in the very largest collective bargaining situations and comparing them with results of the preceding bargaining round. For the current calendar year the Labor Department has identified eleven major bargaining situations where the settlements cover 50,000 or more workers.[8] These settlements affect many workers because of the form of the bargaining arrangement, that is, either a master agreement covering many employers or pattern bargaining where industry employers sign separate but very similar agreements. By the end of November agreements had been reached in ten of the eleven situations.

Summary data on the eleven are presented in tables 4 and 5. Combined they affect about 1.5 million workers, or less than 2 percent of total wage and salary employment. Since 1982 is a heavy bargaining year, this comparatively modest employment total illustrates the decentralized nature of U.S. collective bargaining. Only four of the eleven affect more than 100,000 workers.

Major agreements in the U.S. typically last more than one year. Of the ten that have been negotiated, eight are three-year agreements, one is a two-year agreement (in petroleum), and one is for 2.5 years (in autos). Only in autos is the current agreement significantly shorter than the (three-year) agreement signed in the preceding bargaining round.[9] Multiyear contracts continue to predominate.

Negotiated wage increases in these situations have been much smaller in 1982 than in the preceding round. In table 4 columns (5) and (6) compare annualized percentage wage increases in the current and previous settlement and show that nine of the ten were smaller in 1982. The settlement in men's and boy's clothing is the lone exception, and it is only modestly larger, 6.5 versus 6.1 percent in 1979. An employment-weighted average of the ten agreements was 11.2 percent in the preceding round and 6.1 percent in 1982, slightly more than half of the preceding settlements.

These data provide dramatic evidence of sharply lower 1982 wage settlements, supporting the accounts in the popular media of union wage concessions. Especially notable are the settlements in meat packing, trucking, autos, rubber, and California food processing which are 4 to 7 percent lower than the previous agreements. However, none of the 1982 wage agreements stipulate a wage freeze over the life of the contract. The smallest wage increase averages 4.2 percent, and the remainder fall within a rather narrow range from 5.4 to 8.0 percent.

To summarize, the 1982 agreements, while sharply lower than their predecessors, are not inconsequential. In fact, their average is not much smaller than the average wage increase of 1981IV-1982II summarized in table 3. Thus, the increased relative wage differentials achieved by large unions like the auto workers, teamsters, and the rubber workers during the 1970s will not be significantly eroded by the current settlements. It appears that their near-term wage growth may roughly approximate economywide wage growth.

Columns (2)-(6) of table 5 provide more details on the 1982 contract concessions. Multiyear agreements negotiated in the very largest bargaining situations typically call for both scheduled (or noncontingent) wage increases and cost-of-living (COL or contingent) adjustments. Of the eleven situations noted in tables 4 and 5, all but one (petroleum) have cost-of-living provisions.[10] For the others there could be wage concessions affecting noncontingent increases, contingent increases, or both.

Concessions in scheduled wage increases have occurred in five of the ten agreements. In four (meat packing, trucking, autos, and rubber) the 1982 contract calls for no scheduled increases over the life of the agreement. No attempt was made to identify situations where the noncontingent increases (usually paid at the start of each year in multiyear agreements) were much smaller than in the previous round, but clearly they were smaller in the petroleum industry.

Two types of concessions in COLAs have occurred. The trucking agreement revised the number of COLA reviews (from two to one per year) and actually reduced the 1982 payment (originally due under the preceding contract) from 72 cents to 47 cents. In two others (meat packing and autos) there has been a deferral of COL increases, but the computation procedure for escalator adjustments was not changed. None of the other seven had its escalator clause changed. From this it would appear that unions have been loath to give up the principal of contingent (inflation-related) wage payments.

A paramount union bargaining objective has always been "to take wages out of competition." In practice union bargainers have

TABLE 4

OUTCOMES OF SELECTED COLLECTIVE BARGAINING AGREEMENTS
NEGOTIATED IN 1982[a]

| Employer Group (1) | Union (2) | Number of Workers[a] (000's) (3) |
|---|---|---|
| Petroleum companies | Oil, chemical, and atomic workers | 50.0 |
| Meat packing companies | United food and commercial workers | 50.0 |
| Men's and boy's clothing manufacturers association | Clothing and textile workers | 56.0 |
| Trucking Management, Inc. | International Brotherhood of Teamsters | 300.0 |
| Automobile manufacturers | Auto workers | 628.0 |
| Rubber manufacturers | Rubber workers | 60.0 |
| Ladies apparel manufacturers | Ladies garment workers | 52.0 |
| Electrical equipment manufacturers (G.E., Westinghouse) | Various electrical unions | 120.0 |
| California food processors | International Brotherhood of Teamsters | 60.0 |
| Cotton garment manufacturers | Clothing and textile workers | 60.0 |
| Farm and construction equipment manufacturers | Auto workers | 106.0 |

a. Agreements affecting 50,000 or more workers. Estimates of worker totals were taken from table 3 in Mary Anne Andrews and David Schlein, "Bargaining Calendar Will Be Heavy in 1982," *Monthly Labor Review* (December 1981), pp. 21-31. Information on the agreements is based on summaries that have appeared in various issues of *Current Wage Developments*.

TABLE 4 (continued)

| Settlement Date and Contract Duration (4) | Annualized Percentage Wage Increases[b] | |
| --- | --- | --- |
| | *Previous Settlement* (5) | *1982 Settlement* (6) |
| January, 24 mo. | 11.0 | 8.0 |
| January, 36 mo. | 12.4 | 5.4[c] |
| March, 36 mo. | 6.1 | 6.5[c] |
| March, 37 mo. | 11.5 | 5.8[c] |
| March, 30.5 mo. | 12.3[d] | 5.8[e] |
| April, 36 mo. | 12.9[f] | 6.6[g] |
| June, 36 mo. | 8.3 | 7.4[c] |
| July, 36 mo. | 9.7 | 7.2[h] |
| July, 36 mo. | 8.3 | 4.2[c] |
| Sept., 36 mo. | 8.4 | 6.6 |
| Oct. | 11.2 | – |

b. Estimated by the author.

c. Based on an assumed inflation rate of 8 percent for the life of the contract.

d. 1979 settlements at Ford and GM.

e. Settlements at Ford and GM. Cost-of-living adjustments scheduled for 1982 are deferred 18 months, but are then to be paid under the 1982 agreement. Estimated adjustments are based on an assumed inflation rate of 7.5 percent, the rate used by the parties in costing the agreement.

f. Excludes the settlement at Uniroyal.

g. Based on an assumed inflation rate of 7 percent, the rate used by the parties in costing the agreement. Excludes the settlement at Uniroyal in February 1982.

h. Based on an assumed inflation rate of 6 percent, the rate used by the parties in costing the agreement of major agreements.

i. The average excludes workers at International Harvester, who renegotiated their 1979 contract in May 1982.

TABLE 5

DETAILED OUTCOMES OF SELECTED COLLECTIVE BARGAINING AGREEMENTS
NEGOTIATED IN 1982[a]

| | 1982 Settlements | | | | |
|---|---|---|---|---|---|
| Employer Group (1) | Scheduled Wage Concessions (2) | Cost-of Living Concessions (3) | Deviations from Industry Pattern (4) | Other Union Concessions (5) | Early Contract Reopening (6) |
| **Petroleum companies** | No | Not applicable, no-cost-of-living clause | No | No | No |
| **Meat packing companies** | Yes, no scheduled increases | Yes, deferral of COLAs | Yes, local union wage concessions | Yes, lower starting wages | Yes |
| **Men's and boy's clothing manufacturers association** | No | No | No | No | No |
| **Trucking Management, Inc.** | Yes, no scheduled increases | Yes, fewer reviews, partial diversion of first COLA | Yes, local union wage concessions | Yes, work rule changes | Yes |
| **Automobile manufacturers** | Yes, no scheduled increases | Yes, deferral of COLAs | Yes, Chrysler workers paid below scale | Yes, no personal holidays, lower scale for new workers | Yes |

TABLE 5 (continued)

| Detailed SIC Code (7) | Industry Employment: Date and Number of Workers[b] (000's) | | Recent Reduction in Extent of Unionization[c] (10) |
| | Previous Settlement (8) | 1982 Settlement (9) | |
|---|---|---|---|
| 291 | Dec. 1979, 104.8 | Dec. 1981, 102.9 | – |
| 2011 | Aug. 1979, 132.6 | Dec. 1981, 126.5 | Yes |
| 231 | Sept. 1980, 67.9 | Feb. 1982, 67.2 | – |
| 421-3 | March 1979, 1,093.2 | Feb. 1982, 962.2 | Yes |
| 371 | Sept. 1979, 751.5 | March 1982, 527.4 | – |

TABLE 5 (continued)

DETAILED OUTCOMES OF SELECTED COLLECTIVE BARGAINING AGREEMENTS
NEGOTIATED IN 1982[a]

| | 1982 Settlements | | | | |
|---|---|---|---|---|---|
| Employer Group (1) | Scheduled Wage Concessions (2) | Cost-of Living Concessions (3) | Deviations from Industry Pattern (4) | Other Union Concessions (5) | Early Contract Reopening (6) |
| Rubber manufacturers | Yes, no scheduled increases | No | Yes, Uniroyal workers and other locals paid below scale | Yes, work rule changes | No |
| Ladies apparel manufacturers | No | No | No | No | No |
| Electrical equipment manufacturers (G.E., Westinghouse) | No | No | No | No | No |
| California food processors | Yes, no first-year increases | No | No | No | No |
| Cotton garment manufacturers | No | No | No | No | No |
| Farm and construction equipment manufacturers | – | – | Yes, Harvester workers paid below scale | – | No |

TABLE 5 (continued)

| Detailed SIC Code (7) | Industry Employment: Date and Number of Workers[b] (000's) | | Recent Reduction in Extent of Unionization[c] (10) |
| | Previous Settlement (8) | 1982 Settlement (9) | |
|---|---|---|---|
| 301 | March 1979, 93.0 | March 1982, 69.5 | Yes |
| 2335 | May 1979, 141.2 | May 1982, 111.4 | – |
| 36 | June 1979, 1,407.3 | June 1982, 1,239.6 | – |
| 2033 | June 1979, 71.5 | June 1982, 52.2 | – |
| 232 | Aug. 1979, 315.0 | Aug. 1982, 266.5 | – |
| 3523 | Sept. 1979, 115.9 | Sept. 1982, 67.1 | – |

a. Agreements affecting 50,000 or more workers. Estimates of worker totals were taken from table 3 in Mary Anne Andrews and David Schlein, "Bargaining Calendar Will Be Heavy in 1982," *Monthly Labor Review* (December 1981), pp. 21-31. Information on the agreements is based on summaries that have appeared in various issues of *Current Wage Developments*.

b. Based on production worker employee estimates published in *Employment and Earnings*. Employment estimates are not seasonally adjusted. They refer to the month prior to the agreement.

c. Based on author's judgement.

tried to achieve common rates of pay for union members employed by different companies and by different plants of a single company in the manufacture of a common product. Concerns about plant closings and corporate bankruptcies have recently caused unions to explicitly consider wage-employment trade-offs in negotiating new contracts. One result in the 1982 agreements has been to allow wage provisions at individual plants and/or entire companies to deviate from the general union wage pattern in the industry. Major deviations are identified in column (4) of table 5. Workers at Chrysler, Uniroyal, and Harvester are now paid below their respective industry scales, and local deviations are also present for companies in meat packing, trucking, and other companies in the rubber industry. These deviations represent a major departure from agreements reached in earlier bargaining rounds.[11]

Lower wage settlements in 1982 are undoubtedly a reflection of union concerns for job security. Changes in work rules, fringe benefit concessions, and deviations from scale have all occurred in the current bargaining round.[12] To give more insight into what is motivating the increased job security concerns, columns (7)-(10) in table 5 show information on current industry employment changes and changes in unionization. Between July of 1979 and July of 1982 production worker employment in manufacturing fell by 15.7 percent. In five of the industries where 1982 settlements have taken place industry employment fell by larger percentages, and in three more employment reductions exceeded 10 percent.[13] The business cycle and import competition have both contributed to employment reductions in the auto and apparel industries. Nonunion competition has further reduced the number of union jobs in meat packing, trucking, and rubber. Although it is not possible to estimate how many union jobs have been lost, it is clear that the number has been unusually large in recent years, and that the losses have contributed to smaller settlements in 1982.

To summarize tables 4 and 5, at least four comments can be made regarding the change-in-wage-bargaining hypothesis. (1) There has been a dramatic reduction in the size of new collective bargaining agreements. (2) The reduction, to an average of about 6 percent per year, places these wage increases in the same general range as the broader wage indices shown in table 3. (3) Several aspects of the 1982 settlements suggest important changes in union wage determination (settlements that omit noncontingent increases, deferral of COLAs, significant deviations from industry scales at individual companies and plants, and other concessions). (4) Two of the most important institutional features of union wage setting, multiyear contracts and escalator clauses, emerged with only minor modifications in these 1982 agreements. Thus, the potential for larger future union wage increases and fast union wage responses to future inflationary episodes was practically unaffected by collective bargaining developments in 1982. Actual realization of these possibilities, however, would depend on a return to full employment and/ or rapid changes in the inflation rate.

The retardation of union wage changes has been significant and measurable. The implications for overall wage inflation, however, could be exaggerated. In the first half of 1982 average union wages have been rising at a rate of about 6 percent per year. This certainly will help relieve inflationary cost pressures in several industries, but it will not act as a strong signal for major reductions in nonunion wage changes. Nonunion wage changes are also increasing at about this rate (see columns (6) and (9) in table 3). For the present, union settlements are certainly not providing independent inflationary impulses in the labor market.

## Wage Equation Forecasts for 1981 and 1982

The modified Phillips curve explanation of the recent slowdown can be evaluated by analyzing the predictive accuracy of macro wage equations. To do this several widely used wage equations will be examined for the six quarters from 1981I to 1982II. In each case the actual values of all explanatory variables have been used to produce forecasts of money wage increases.[14] The exercise is useful for assessing how well wage equations have been tracking wage developments in recent quarters. If the modified Phillips curve provides a sufficient explanation for recent developments, equation residuals would be expected to average zero. Under both the change-in-wage-bargaining hypothesis and credible restrictive monetary policy hypothesis, however, negative residuals would be expected to predominate, that is, increases would be smaller than predicted by a modified Phillips curve.

Table 6 presents summary data on the performance of four macro equations that explain percentage increases in hourly compensation (wages plus fringe benefits). Details of the individual equation specifications are varied, but they contain several common ele-

TABLE 6

ACTUAL AND PREDICTED COMPENSATION GROWTH, 1981I TO 1982II[a]

| Dependent Variable | Fed Model[b] Private Nonfarm Business Compensation per Hour | BEA Model[b] Private Nonfarm Business Compensation per Hour | Wharton Model[b,c] Private Nonfarm Hourly Earning in Eight Sectors, Adjusted for Supplements | DRI Model[b] Private Nonfarm Earnings Index Adjusted for Supplements |
|---|---|---|---|---|
| | | *Actual Increases* | | |
| 1981I | 11.8 | 11.7 | 11.7 | 11.7 |
| 1981II | 7.0 | 7.0 | 5.8 | 7.4 |
| 1981III | 9.2 | 9.1 | 9.4 | 9.0 |
| 1981IV | 7.5 | 7.4 | 8.3 | 7.4 |
| 1982I | 7.8 | 7.4 | 12.0 | 7.5 |
| 1982II | 5.9 | 5.7 | 3.4 | 6.0 |
| | | *Predicted Increases* | | |
| 1981I | 12.9 | 11.7 | 9.6 | – |
| 1981II | 10.5 | 10.0 | 9.0 | – |
| 1981III | 9.9 | 9.5 | 8.8 | – |
| 1981IV | 9.1 | 9.1 | 8.4 | – |
| 1982I | 8.4 | 9.1 | 7.7 | – |
| 1982II | 6.7 | 8.2 | 6.8 | – |
| | | *Residuals* | | |
| 1981I | – 1.1 | .0 | 2.1 | – |
| 1981II | – 3.5 | – 3.0 | – 3.2 | – |
| 1981III | – .7 | – .4 | .6 | – |
| 1981IV | – 1.6 | – 1.7 | – .1 | – |
| 1982I | – .6 | – 1.7 | 4.3 | – |
| 1982II | – .8 | – 2.5 | – 3.4 | – |
| Standard error[d] | 1.30 | 1.47 | .77[c] | .78 |
| | | *Average Residuals* | | |
| 1981I-1981III | – 1.77 | – 1.13 | – .17 | – .80 |
| 1981IV-1982II | – 1.00 | – 1.97 | .27 | – 1.50 |
| Standard deviation of average expected error[e] | .75 | .85 | .44 | .45 |
| Ratio to average expected error | | | | |
| 1981I-1981III | – 2.35 | – 1.33 | – .39 | – 1.77 |
| 1981IV-1982II | – 1.33 | – 2.32 | .61 | – 3.33 |

ments.[15] Unemployment and recent actual inflation are explanatory variables in all equations. Typically unemployment enters as a demographically adjusted rate or as the deviation between the overall rate and the "full employment" unemployment rate. Price changes enter with lags of from two to three years. Other explanatory variables in individual equations include the minimum wage, employer payroll taxes, incomes policy dummy variables, and unemployment insurance payments.

Actual compensation has been increasing at slower rates in 1982 than in 1981, a pattern previously observed in the wage data of table 3.[16] All equations predict slowdowns in compensation growth during these six quarters. Since actual inflation was declining and unemployment increasing in this period, these time paths are exactly what would be expected from modified Phillips curves. Because actual price changes enter the regression equations with rather long lags (two to three years) the short-run variability of actual inflation rates is smoothed out by the lag structure on the price inflation variables. By the second quarter of 1982 predicted compensation increases ranged from half to two-thirds of the predictions for 1981I.

The predictive accuracy of the individual equations is examined in the bottom panels of table 6. The residuals displayed in table 6 suggest a Scotch verdict on the modified Phillips curve interpretation. Of the eighteen that appear, fourteen are negative, that is, actual changes are smaller than predicted changes. When they are averaged over three quarter intervals (to be compatible with the available detail from the DRI forecasts), seven of the eight averages are negative. The averages, however, are not large for all equations. Some of the averages are small in comparison to the standard errors for the equations that appear immediately below the forecast errors.

---

a. All equations were fitted using quarterly data. Actual increases, predicted increases, and residuals are percentages measured at annual rates.

b. Equations obtained from research staffs that produce these model forecasts. Respectively these are the Board of Governors of the Federal Reserve Board (FED), the Bureau of Economics Analysis of the U.S. Commerce Department (BEA), Wharton Econometric Forecasting Associates (Wharton), and Data Resources Incorporated (DRI).

c. Data from the Wharton model are fixed weight averages of data from eight private nonfarm industries. Wage bill weights were used to combine the industry data.

d. The standard error of the underlying equation expressed at an annualized percentage rate.

e. Standard error of the equation divided by the square root of three. Three is the number of observations in the averaging period.

Thus, even though the equations have been overpredicting wage increases in recent quarters, the average size of the overpredictions has not been consistently large relative to the basic error variances of the underlying equations. A rough test of the eight averages indicates that three were significantly negative at the .05 level and one more at the .10 level.[17] Thus, there is some evidence of a recent deceleration in excess of the equation predictions.[18]

To summarize, recent compensation increases have definitely decelerated, but not by too much more than would be predicted by a modified Phillips curve. Higher unemployment and reduced price inflation have been mainly responsible for the recent deceleration in money wage inflation. Although equation predictions account for most of the downward movement in compensation growth, the pattern of prediction errors is suggestive of additional downward pressure on compensation growth. This residual pattern is consistent with additional effects due to a credible restrictive monetary policy and/or the effects of changes in wage determination under collective bargaining. Of the various hypotheses examined here, however, the modified Phillips curve carries by far the largest weight in explaining the recent slowdown.

# CHAPTER 6

# PROSPECTS FOR WAGE INFLATION IN 1982–1983

There are several reasons to expect modest rates of money wage inflation in late 1982 and in 1983. As noted, wage gains started to decelerate noticeably in 1981IV and even more in the first half of 1982. At least four separate factors can be identified which will contribute to moderate wage gains in the upcoming period: (1) the low level of overall resource utilization, (2) likely price developments, (3) the stance of monetary policy, and (4) likely collective bargaining developments.

Macro resource utilization currently stands at an all time low for the post-World War II period. The overall unemployment rate, which was 9.5 percent in 1982II, averaged 9.9 percent in 1982III. Under any foreseeable real GNP growth projection there is no way this rate will fall below 8 percent by the fourth quarter of 1983. Thus, inflationary pressures associated with excess demand in the labor market will be practically nonexistent throughout 1983. Current and lagged effects of the unemployment increases between 1981IV and 1982III will operate with especially strong force in 1982IV and 1983I. Even if there were a vigorous rebound of real GNP, overall unemployment would still be in the 8.0-8.5 percent range at the end of 1983.

Table 3 made a distinction between movements in the all items CPI and the special CPI index. Food, energy, and housing, the items accounting for differences in the two indexes, are likely to exhibit continued low inflation rates throughout the rest of 1982 and early 1983. Although home mortgage interest rates (and other interest rates) will be high by historic standards throughout the remainder of 1982, they have been trending downward and will continue down-

ward for the next two quarters. Thus, mortgage interest rates will
not contribute to inflation in the CPI as it is currently measured.
Abundant supplies of petroleum have been available throughout the
first three quarters of 1982 and will undoubtedly be available for
the next three quarters. A scheduled decontrol of natural gas will
cause a 20 percent increase in the price of this energy source in the
winter of 1982-1983. The effect of this increase should be quite modest, perhaps a .4 to .6 percent increase in the overall CPI. Fall 1982
fuel oil inventories are not large by historic standards. If the winter
is exceptionally cold, existing stocks could be drawn down rapidly
with obvious implications for fuel oil prices. The fall 1982 harvest
of food grains has been very large. Large stocks of agricultural products ensure near-term price moderation in this sector. Thus, of the
three volatile markets, only energy appears to have any independent
inflationary potential for the winter of 1982-1983.

Although some shifts appear to be occurring, monetary policy
is likely to retain a relatively restrictive stance throughout the rest
of 1982 and in 1983. This will continue to exert downward pressure
on resource utilization and inflationary expectations. The effects of
restrictive policy operating through both of these channels will be
a third force inhibiting inflation in the near future.

Another favorable development in the labor market is the number of wage concessions recently negotiated in major collective bargaining agreements and the likelihood of more "concession bargaining"
in 1983. Concessions by members of the auto workers' and teamsters'
unions directly affect more than 800,000 workers covered by highly
visible key agreements. As noted, the new contracts by both unions
call for no fixed wage increases during 1982 as well as lower and/
or deferred cost-of-living increases. Wage concessions in the meat
packing, airline, and rubber industries have already occurred. These
concessions will lead to more modest negotiated wage increases
throughout 1982 and 1983 than the 9.5 percent increase effective
during 1981. It also is very probable that wage concessions will be
made by the united steelworkers when their contracts are renegotiated. Although the size of the effects are not known, spillovers to
other union agreements and to nonunion wages would further en-
hance the effects of the recent and possible future union wage concessions.[1]

Thus, factors operating in labor markets and products markets
as well as monetary policy will all contribute to low rates of wage
and price inflation during the remainder of 1982 and throughout

1983. Although the depth of the current downturn cannot be predicted with certainty, the degree of economic slack currently existing will continue to inhibit wage and price increases during all of 1983. The foreseeable exogenous sources of inflationary impulses in this period will be the natural gas price increases slated for the winter of 1982-1983 and possibly some increases in fuel oil prices.

# NOTES

1. The inflation rates refer to annual average increases in the all items CPI, while the unemployment rates refer to all persons 16 and older.

NOTES TO CHAPTER 2

1. The 1979-1981 period is considered a single episode in the present discussion.

2. One way to approximate the catch-up response of money wages to lagged inflation is to subtract half of the preceding year's rate of price inflation from observed money wage changes. When this was done, the "adjusted" wage change percentages for the 1969-1970, 1974-1975, and 1979-1980 periods were respectively 3.5 and 3.8 percent, 4.9 and 6.2 percent, and 4.3 and 4.1 percent. Most of the wage acceleration observed in figure 1 is explained by the catch-up response to lagged price changes.

NOTES TO CHAPTER 3

1. Table 1 shows data from four distinct U.S. Labor Department-BLS series: the fixed weight hourly earnings index (HEI) (columns (1)-(3)); the Wage Developments in Manufacturing (WDM) data (columns (4)-(6)); the employment cost index (ECI) (columns (7)-(9)); and the effective wage changes negotiated in major collective bargaining agreements (column (10)). Since interest is centered on money wage changes that have occurred within each year, December to December changes (rather than annual averages) have been used for both the HEI and the ECI. The other two series already measure wage changes occurring within each year. For measuring wage rate changes free of various mix effects the ECI is probably the best series, but it is available only since 1975. The hourly earnings index is the only series available for all seventeen years covered by table 1. Note also that none of the data include fringe benefit changes, an increasingly important part of the total compensation package. Each of these series is described in U.S. Department of Labor, Bureau of Labor Statistics, *BLS Handbook of Methods*, Bulletin 1910 (Washington, D.C.: Government Printing Office, 1976). For some critical comments about the usefulness of the various wage series see part III of Wayne Vroman, "Union Contracts and Overall Wage Changes," Working Paper 1467-1 (Washington, D.C.: The Urban Institute, 1981).

2. The wage data which enter the hourly earnings index (columns (1), (2), and (3) of table 1) do not distinguish union from nonunion workers. The major private

41

nonfarm industries, however, fall into two quite distinct unionization groups. Data assembled by Richard Freedman and James Medoff, "New Estimates of Private Sector Unionism in the U.S.," *Industrial and Labor Relations Review* (January 1979), pp. 143-174, indicate that more than half of production workers in mining, construction, manufacturing, transportation, and public utilities are covered by collective bargaining agreements. In contrast, fewer than 30 percent of production workers in trade, finance, and services are covered by union agreements. For the 1968-70-72 period, years examined by Freedman and Medoff, production worker unionization rates averaged .63 and .17 respectively in the two sets of industries. Columns (2) and (3) in table 1 show average wage changes for the two combinations of the major nonfarm industries. Rapid union wage increases would be reflected in the wage increases of industries with high unionization rates. The technique of grouping industries as in columns (2) and (3) to make inferences about union wage behavior has ample precedent. See chapter 3 in Daniel Mitchell, *Union, Wages and Inflation* (Washington, D.C.: The Brookings Institution, 1980) for an application using hourly earnings data from 3-digit SIC industries grouped by degree unionization.

3. It should be observed that merit pay increases, year end bonuses, and other nonscheduled wage increases are omitted from the data in columns (4)-(6). Because nonscheduled increases are more important for nonunion workers than for union workers, this omission biases downward the estimated wage increases for nonunion workers. Unfortunately, there are no data to indicate the size of this downward bias. Note that in the 1965-1967 period, nonunion wage gains exceeded union gains in these data.

4. Compare columns (2) with (3) and (10) with (1) in the bottom two lines of table 1.

5. Using the technique of comparing average hourly earnings in selected (3-digit) highly unionized industries with those in less unionized industries, Daniel Mitchell concluded that union wages grew more rapidly than nonunion wages between 1953 and 1976. In his comparisons (table 3.1, p. 78) it appears that the union wage growth differential was largest in the 1968-1976 period (Mitchell, *Union, Wages and Inflation*).

6. This sentence does not convey a sense for the wide variety of escalator arrangements in union wage contracts. More details on COL formulas and yields are presented in H. M. Douty, "Cost-of-Living Escalator Clauses and Inflation," Council of Wage and Price Stability Staff Report (Washington, D.C.: Government Printing Office, August 1975); and Wayne Vroman, "The Responsiveness of Money Wage Rates to Price Changes," Working Paper 1267-5 (Washington, D.C.: The Urban Institute, 1982).

7. Statements about changes in real wages obviously depend on the choice of the price index used to deflate money wage increases. When the column (1) wage changes were deflated by the consumer expenditures deflator from the national income accounts (fourth quarter to fourth quarter changes), real wages in the major agreements remained roughly constant during 1973-1974 and 1978-1980.

NOTES TO CHAPTER 4

1. Wage and price changes are measured from quarter-to-quarter endpoints and expressed at annual percentage rates. Except for unemployment, all series in the table are based on seasonally unadjusted data. Unadjusted data were used for two reasons: (1) changes in the unadjusted CPI cause other COL increases in union wages and (2) of the three wage series, only the hourly earnings index is published on a seasonally adjusted basis.

2. Rapid price deceleration in the 1981IV-1982II quarters is also apparent when the GNP deflators are examined. Annualized rates of increase in the GNP and per-

sonal consumption (PCE) deflators in the three quarters were about 4 percent below
the averages for the seven preceding quarters: 5.9 versus 9.6 percent in the GNP
deflator and 5.2 versus 9.3 percent in the PCE deflator.

3. Since the hourly earnings index data are published on a seasonally adjusted
basis, the adjusted data could also be examined. Increases in the all industry series
during 1981IV-1982II (not shown in table 3) averaged 6.3 percent compared to 9.2
percent during the seven preceding quarters. In these data the recent slowdown was
somewhat larger in the low union industries, i.e., from 8.8 to 5.6 percent compared
to a decline from 9.4 to 7.1 percent in high union industries. Although the slowdown
has been larger in low union industries (3.2 versus 2.3 percent), it is clearly apparent
in highly unionized industries as well.

4. Columns (8) and (9) again illustrate the contrasting seasonal patterns of
union and nonunion wage increases. In the first quarter of each year nonunion wage
increases are the larger of the two, while union increases are consistently larger in
all second, third, and fourth quarters. Also, observe that the seasonal acceleration
of union wage gains between 1982I and 1982II was especially small relative to the
preceding two years. This would be expected in a collective bargaining environment
characterized by union concessions in several major agreements.

5. Details of several large 1982 bargaining agreements are given in chapter 5.

6. Real GNP fell 2.5 percent between 1980I and 1980II. It fell by 2.6 percent
between 1981III and 1982I.

7. The modified Phillips curve explains wage inflation in terms of unemployment and the (lagged or expected) inflation rate. In the so-called accelerationist
version of the relationship the inflation rate has a coefficient of unity. Actual wage
inflation responds to expected (or lagged) price inflation with a unitary elasticity.

NOTES TO CHAPTER 5

1. This section of the paper will focus on money wage growth while the rate
of price inflation will be taken as a given. This is a partial analysis in that the role
of wage-price feedback in the inflationary process will not be examined. Although
the resulting analysis is partial in nature, it has the advantage of focusing just on
developments in the labor market. To conduct a parallel analysis of recent price
inflation would substantially increase the scope of the present paper. Thus, attention
will be focused on the time path of money wage changes given the historic realization
of price developments.

2. A recent issue of *Challenge* magazine features three articles; one by Freedman arguing that fundamental change is taking place, and rejoinders by Mitchell
and Dunlop. See Audrey Freedman, "A Fundamental Change in Wage Bargaining,"
*Challenge* (July-August 1982), pp. 14-17; Daniel Mitchell, "Gain-Sharing: An Anti-
Inflation Reform," *Challenge* (July-August 1982), pp. 18-25; and John Dunlop, "Working Toward Consensus," *Challenge* (July-August 1982), pp. 26-34.

3. William Fellner, "The Valid Case of the Rationality Hypothesis in the Theory
of Expectations," *Journal of Money Credit and Banking* (November 1980), pp. 763-
787.

4. The targets were 3.5 to 6.0 percent in 1981 and 2.5 to 5.0 percent in 1982.
These are annual growth rates for M1 (formally M1B). Actual growth of M1 was 5.0
percent in 1981 and through August of 1982 growth has been at a 5.6 percent annual
rate. Although the growth targets have been achieved in 1981 and 1982, there has
been substantial short-run variability in monetary growth rates. Economists from
the monetarist school remain highly critical of the Fed because of this short-run
money stock variability.

5. The Livingston data are expected rates as measured by the Carlson ad-
justment to the raw survey data. These data were obtained from the Philadelphia

Fed. Questions are also asked about 6- and 18-month expected inflation rates in this survey. The Michigan data were obtained from the Survey Research Center of the Institute for Social Research. These data are to be revised later in 1982, but the revisions will have only minor effects on the mean expected inflation rate.

6. Recent analysis of the determinants of inflationary expectations includes Stephen Figlewski and Paul Wachtel, "The Formation of Inflationary Expectations" *Review of Economics and Statistics* (February 1981), pp. 1-10; Edward Gramlich, "Models of Inflationary Expectations Formation: A Comparison of Household and Economist Forecasts," University of Michigan, mimeo (May 1982); Donald Mullineaux, "On Testing for Rationality: Another Look at the Livingston Price Expectations Data," *Journal of Political Economy* (April 1978), pp. 329-336; Donald Mullineaux, "Inflation Expectations and Money Growth in the United States," *American Economic Review* (March 1980), pp. 149-161; and James Pesando, "A Note on the Rationality of the Livingston Price Expectations," *Journal of Political Economy* (August 1975), pp. 849-858. Gramlich's paper explicitly compares the sensitivity of empirical results using both the Livingston and the Michigan data.

7. Empirical studies of inflationary expectations also cast doubt on the rational expectations hypothesis, i.e., that expected inflation responds to actual inflation with a unitary elasticity. See Figlewski and Wachtel, "The Formation of Inflationary Expectations." They conclude that expectations are formed in an adaptive manner. In Gramlich, "Models of Inflationary Expectations Formation," the author finds that most of the empirical results using both price expectations series are inconsistent with rational expectations.

8. These agreements are identified in table 3 of Mary Anne Andrews and David Schlein, "Bargaining Calendar Will Be Heavy in 1982," *Monthly Labor Review* (December 1981), pp. 21-31.

9. Note, however, that the actual duration of 1982 agreements can differ from the durations specified at the time of contract negotiations. Early reopenings in meat packing and autos caused actual contract durations to be significantly shorter in the preceding round than the durations agreed to when these contracts were negotiated in 1979. It seems likely that the 1982 agreements in farm implements will be significantly shorter than 36 months. Agreements of 21-month duration would keep these in tandem with the expiration of the auto agreements in the fall of 1984.

10. Traditionally, the cost-of-living adjustments have been very small in the three apparel industry settlements identified in table 4 and in the California food processors' agreements. Recall from table 2 that COL adjustments have accounted for about 30 percent of wage increases negotiated in major bargaining situations in recent years.

11. Downward deviations also present problems in trying to assess the size of 1982 agreements in individual industries. Column (6) shows the size of pattern setting agreements. All-industry averages would be somewhat lower if the effects of these concessions were included.

12. Several important concessions appear in column (3) of table 5.

13. The five were in autos, rubber, ladies apparel, food processing, and farm equipment where the decreases were 29.8, 25.3, 21.1, 27.0, and 42.1 percent respectively. Decreases of from 10 to 15.7 percent occurred in trucking, electrical equipment, and cotton garment manufacturing; 12.0, 11.9, and 15.4 percent respectively.

14. Note that the analysis is partial in nature because it takes the path of actual price increases to be a given. It is possible that there is a direct effect of restrictive monetary policy on actual price increases, i.e., the so-called credibility effect. Macro policy effects that operate directly on prices are not included in this analysis.

15. The equations are available from the author.

16. Even though the compensation data are seasonally adjusted, first quarter increases exceed those of later quarters. Increases in employer social insurance con-

tributions occur in the first quarter, and these increases influence the quarterly changes even in seasonally adjusted data. When corresponding quarters of 1981 and 1982 are compared, it is also clear that actual compensation increases have been declining.

17. As a test of "significance" of the averages, each was compared to the expected "standard error" for three observations, i.e., the standard error for the equations divided by the square of three (the number of observations in the averages). Three of the ratios exceeded two in absolute value, which would be required by a two-tailed test at the .05 level of significance while one exceeds 1.68 which is required for significance at the .10 level. This then is some evidence for significant negative residuals in this period. Note that this is only a rough test. No allowance has been made for the deviations of the explanatory variables from their sample means. Recognition of these deviations would increase the standard errors of the equations' predictions.

18. The forecasts displayed in table 6 represent a sampling from the large scale models. Clearly there are other wage and compensation equations which could also be consulted. For example, in a recent paper by Robert Gordon, "Inflation, Flexible Exchange Rates, and the Natural Rate of Unemployment," in Martin Bailey, ed., *Workers, Jobs and Inflation* (Washington, D.C.: The Brookings Institution, 1982), pp. 89-152, the author includes an analysis of both wage and price behavior through the end of 1980. The specification of the wage equation in his paper differs from mainline equations in two important respects: productivity increases are subtracted from money wage increases, and a very long lag (six years) is applied to the price term. When Gordon's equation was used to forecast wage gains, the result was a pattern of declining wage increases for the the six quarters in the 1981I-1982II period. Unlike table 6, however, Gordon's equation consistently overpredicts actual wage increases during these six quarters. Thus, his results are similar to those of table 6 in forecasting a slowdown of wage gains during these quarters but differ in the sign of the prediction errors.

NOTE TO CHAPTER 6

1. Two points should be noted regarding possible wider effects of recent and possible future concessions. First, as Wachter, Hall, and others noted in the April 1982 meetings of the Brookings Panel on Economic Activity, there may not be much of a spillover from concessions. Large wage gains during the 1970s sharply increased the relative wages of the auto workers, steelworkers, rubber workers, coal miners, and teamsters. Other wage and salary workers may be reluctant to now make wage concessions that would perpetuate their lower relative wage position vis-a-vis workers in these very large unions. Second, even after making concessions, workers in the largest situations will receive sizeable wage increases in their current contracts. Average increases of 6 percent per year should not cause much of a further slowdown in other wage increases.

THE CHANGING DOMESTIC PRIORITIES SERIES

In 1982, The Urban Institute began a three-year project to examine shifts in economic and social policies occurring under the Reagan administration. That project is called Changing Domestic Priorities. Its objectives are (1) to monitor and interpret significant shifts in economic and social policy; (2) to determine the actual and likely consequences of these shifts; and (3) to explore the implications and alternatives for future public actions.

*The Reagan Experiment,* the first volume in the Changing Domestic Priorities Series, is followed by detailed paperback studies and a final overview volume. The paperback studies now available are *Housing Assistance for Older Americans: The Reagan Prescription; Medicaid in the Reagan Era: Federal Policy and State Choices;* and *Wage Inflation: Prospects for Deceleration.*

THE URBAN INSTITUTE PRESS · WASHINGTON, D.C.

ISBN 0-87766-320